Fighting Inflation
and Rebuilding A Sound Economy

A Statement by the
Research and
Policy Committee of the
Committee for
Economic Development

September 1980

Library of Congress Cataloging in Publication Data

Committee for Economic Development. Subcommittee on
   Inflation Policy.
   Fighting inflation and rebuilding a sound economy.

   Includes bibliographical references.
   1. United States—Economic policy—1971-
2. Inflation (Finance)—United States.   I. Committee
for Economic Development.   Research and Policy Committee.
II. Title.
HC106.7.C645 1980   338.973   80-21679
ISBN 0-87186-771-0 (lib. bdg.)
ISBN 0-87186-071-6 (pbk.)

First printing: September 1980
Paperbound: $3.00
Library binding: $4.00
Printed in the United States of America by Semline Incorporated
Design: Stead, Young & Rowe, Inc.

COMMITTEE FOR ECONOMIC DEVELOPMENT
477 Madison Avenue, New York, N.Y. 10022
1700 K Street, N.W., Washington, D.C. 20006 80-9831

CONTENTS

Fighting Inflation
and Rebuilding
A Sound Economy

RESPONSIBILITY FOR CED STATEMENTS ON NATIONAL POLICY

The Committee for Economic Development is an independent research and educational organization of two hundred business executives and educators. CED is nonprofit, nonpartisan, and nonpolitical. Its purpose is to propose policies that will help to bring about steady economic growth at high employment and reasonably stable prices, increase productivity and living standards, provide greater and more equal opportunity for every citizen, and improve the quality of life for all. A more complete description of CED is to be found on page 26.

All CED policy recommendations must have the approval of the Research and Policy Committee, trustees whose names are listed on page vii. This Committee is directed under the bylaws to "initiate studies into the principles of business policy and of public policy which will foster the full contribution by industry and commerce to the attainment and maintenance" of the objectives stated above. The bylaws emphasize that "all research is to be thoroughly objective in character, and the approach in each instance is to be from the standpoint of the general welfare and not from that of any special political or economic group." The Committee is aided by a Research Advisory Board of leading social scientists and by a small permanent professional staff.

The Research and Policy Committee is not attempting to pass judgment on any pending specific legislative proposals; its purpose is to urge careful consideration of the objectives set forth in this statement and of the best means of accomplishing those objectives.

Each statement is preceded by extensive discussions, meetings, and exchanges of memoranda. The research is undertaken by a subcommittee, assisted by advisors chosen for their competence in the field under study. The members and advisors of the subcommittee that prepared this statement are listed on page viii.

The full Research and Policy Committee participates in the drafting of findings and recommendations. Likewise, the trustees on the drafting subcommittee vote to approve or disapprove a policy statement, and they share with the Research and Policy Committee the privilege of submitting individual comments for publication, as noted on pages vii and viii and on the appropriate page of the text of the statement.

Except for the members of the Research and Policy Committee and the responsible subcommittee, the recommendations presented herein are not necessarily endorsed by other trustees or by the advisors, contributors, staff members, or others associated with CED.

RESEARCH AND POLICY COMMITTEE

SUBCOMMITTEE ON INFLATION POLICY

ADVISORS TO THE SUBCOMMITTEE

PROJECT DIRECTOR

PROJECT EDITOR

PROJECT STAFF

CED STAFF ADVISORS

Purpose of this Statement

Inflation poses a serious threat to the very foundation of our economy and our society. It was the consensus of the subcommittee that prepared this report that nothing weakens our national confidence or the confidence of our allies more than the inability of the United States to control inflation.

Furthermore, persistent and accelerating inflation has become woven into the fabric of our national life in such a way that it impedes our ability to deal forcefully with such other pressing problems as energy, employment, trade, and defense. In turn, these other major problems have both fueled inflation and increased resistance to moderating prices.

The United States needs an economy that works well and works productively. There should be no higher-priority item on the national economic agenda than that of controlling inflation. Yet inflation has proven stubbornly resistant to national policy remedies.

INTERRELATED PROBLEMS REQUIRE COORDINATED REMEDIES

One reason inflation has proven so intractable is that policy makers tend to approach inflation as a single, separable problem. In fact, our present inflation is but one component in a larger network of economic problems that are themselves difficult to solve and that also tend to worsen inflation and hold down economic performance.

We believe that if this country is to achieve a long-term reduction in inflation and is to rebuild a healthy economy, both government and the public must recognize the interrelated nature of our major economic problems. And we also believe that they must be willing to accept the kinds of solutions that are necessary.

CED's policy studies have been designed to focus on the interplay between a number of our nation's major problems and the long-term, coordinated approach needed to surmount them. CED's recent study of regulation, *Redefining Government's Role in the Market System*, calls for increasing productivity and encouraging growth by reducing distortions and misallocations caused by overregulation. CED's 1980 statement, *Stimulating Technological Progress*, urges a combination of tax, patent, and regulatory reforms to spur innovation, step up capital investment, and improve productivity.Our recent studies in the energy field demonstrate that market pricing of energy will make the greatest contribution to domestic energy production and conservation, to inflation control, and to reducing balance-of-payments deficits. Our continuing support of public-private training and job efforts, growing out of the study *Jobs for the Hard-to-Employ*, is directed both toward furthering social equity and toward improving the performance of the economy by investing in human capital. CED's current study of retirement policy is examining the differing impacts of funded pension systems versus transfer payments on savings and capital investment, as well as on inflation and productivity. CED's succession of urban studies have been developing proposals for how cities can make better use of both public and private labor and capital, thereby increasing economic efficiency and improving social well-being. Our current study of international trade is assessing the impact of industrial policies on long-term productivity, balance of payments, economic growth, and long-term inflation. CED's forthcoming study of productivity will examine the importance of productivity to the U.S. economy, examine the causes of recent productivity deterioration, and present a coordinated picture of actions needed to improve performance in this critical area.

THE NEED FOR ACTION

All these policy studies stressed the importance of a long-term view of improving the U. S. economy. But no long-term goals can be achieved unless policy makers commit themselves to the requisite actions. This is particularly important in the fight against inflation. There is a real danger that as the current slack in the economy continues, policy makers will downplay the need for tough anti-inflation measures in favor of excessively stimulative actions that will slow or halt what little progress has been made in curbing inflation.

Now is the time to begin implementing policies to build up an eroding industrial capacity, to improve productivity, and to restore U. S. competitiveness in world markets. Recovery from this recession should be achieved with measures that shift the current bias that favors consumption and short-term defensive strategies to policies that encourage greater saving, investment, and productivity.

This policy statement offers a number of coordinated steps that combine fiscal and monetary restraint, certain tax adjustments, and selected structural measures which, if taken simultaneously, will slow current inflation, make the economy more resistant to future inflationary pressures, and restore healthy economic growth and adequate job opportunities.

We believe that if the policies recommended in this statement and other needed measures are put into action, this nation will be on the road to achieving a sound economy, a year-by-year reduction in inflation, and eventually, an essential price stability.

A SIGNIFICANT CONTRIBUTION

A list of the members of the Research and Policy Committee, which approved this report, appears on page vii. The members are to be commended for the time and thoughtful consideration they gave to this statement.

We are especially indebted to Ruben F. Mettler for the skill and wisdom he brought to this project as subcommittee chairman and to Frank W. Schiff, CED's vice president and chief economist and project director for this study, for the knowledge and insights he brought to the arduous task of drafting this statement. The subcommittee that was responsible for preparing this report was made up of Trustees, and assisted by advisors, who possess broad depth and experience with the complex issues involved in fighting inflation. A list of subcommittee members and advisors appears on page viii.

Franklin A. Lindsay, *Chairman*
Research and Policy Committee

Fighting
Inflation
and Rebuilding
A Sound
Economy

INTRODUCTION AND SUMMARY

The American economy is in a perilous state.

We suffer from both very serious inflation and sharp recession. The domestic and international consequences are profound. The recession is proving to be one of the deepest since World War II. Although overall inflation rates have receded from their peak levels earlier in the year, they remain very high. At the same time, the underlying inflation rate—the inflation that has become imbedded in increased production costs— has been climbing stubbornly for the past decade and a half, rising from less than 2 percent in the mid-1960s to the present level of around 9 to 10 percent. (See "What Is Inflation," on page 2, and Figure 1, on page 3.)

If no more than a cyclical remission in overall inflation rates is achieved during the current recession, a renewed upsurge in inflation can be expected once the economy recovers. This reacceleration of inflation would once again be starting from a significantly higher base than that which followed the previous recession.

In our view, such a continued ratcheting upward of inflation is simply not acceptable. Temporary reductions in inflation rates during the recession must not lead to a mistaken belief that the fight against inflation can be relaxed. **A central aim of national economic policy should be a progressive, year-by-year reduction in the underlying inflation rate—continuing after the recession has ended—until essential price stability is achieved.**[1]

Continued high inflation is very damaging to the national well-being. Inflation redistributes incomes and wealth in a highly arbitrary and inequitable fashion. Society as a whole loses because of the adverse effects of in-

---

[1]/As noted in our 1976 policy statement *Fighting Inflation and Promoting Growth*, "we continue to believe that the basic objective with respect to prices should be the attainment of price stability, not merely some reduction in the rate of inflation. We identify absence of price inflation with stability in the consumer price index after allowing for the inability of this index fully to reflect quality changes in the production of goods and services. We recognize, moreover, that interim goals for the reduction of inflation under current government programs cannot realistically call for the complete elimination of inflationary tendencies within a very short period of time."

WHAT IS INFLATION?

Some of the controversy surrounding the discussion of inflation stems from confusion over the meaning imputed to the word.

As used in this policy statement, the term *inflation* refers to increases in the general level of prices for goods and services. Such increases represent losses in the general purchasing power of money. The most commonly used measure of U.S. inflation is the consumer price index (CPI), but other measures (such as the gross national product deflator or the personal consumption expenditure component of this deflator) can also be used.

The term *underlying inflation* as used here refers to persistent cost and price increases that have become imbedded in the price structure in the form of rising unit labor and capital costs. This measure of inflation differs from the *overall rate of inflation* (as measured, for example, by the CPI) in that it excludes the direct impact on the CPI of volatile movements in the prices of such items as food and energy, as well as in home mortgage rates. However, price increases from these sources do become incorporated in the underlying inflation rate once they begin to exert an influence on the trend in labor and capital costs. The relative movements of overall inflation rates and of underlying inflation since 1958 are shown in Figure 1.

FIGURE 1

Overall and Underlying Rates of Inflation

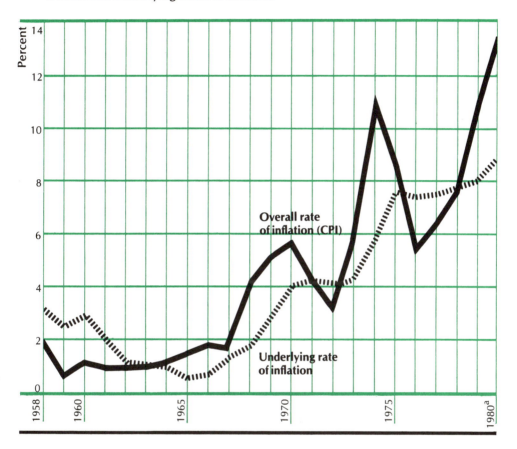

Various alternative measures can be used to depict overall and underlying inflation. In this chart, the overall inflation rate is represented by the consumer price index (CPI). Underlying inflation is represented by the "core rate" concept developed by Data Resources, which measures the weighted average of the trend rates of growth in unit labor and capital costs (with weights equal to the estimated shares of these costs in total value added and with adjustments for productivity growth). For a detailed technical description, see Otto Eckstein and Robin Siegel, "More on Core Inflation," *Data Resources U.S. Review* (June 1979), pp.I.19–I.23.

a/ 1980 figures partly estimated by Data Resources.

SOURCES: U.S. Department of Labor, Bureau of Labor Statistics, and Data Resources, Inc.

flation on productivity, output, and economic growth. Inflation seriously interferes with rational corporate and personal saving and investment decisions, undermines financial markets, exacerbates industrial and social strife, and causes a diversion of the country's productive energies away from long-term productive investment into speculative or defensive efforts.

The corrosive inflation and sharp recession are interrelated with many other problems: declining productivity, lagging capital investment, serious deficiencies in our ability to compete effectively in international markets, and wide disparities in the economic health of different areas of the country and sectors of the economy. Moreover, the value of the dollar has been adversely affected by the intensity and persistence of our domestic inflation, and this, in turn, has been a significant contributor to that inflation.

Devising an economic policy strategy to cope with all these problems is a task of highest priority. The decisions made or not made now and in the year ahead will have a profound impact on the long-term prospects for our economy.

The economic policy choices will not be easy. Some proposed short-run remedies are likely to hurt long-run prospects; conversely, some policies aimed at promoting longer-run economic health can aggravate short-term difficulties. Conflicting pressures could trigger a series of ad hoc government efforts to relieve each point of pressure. The result could further exacerbate inflation.

A major risk is that recession will lead to an abandonment of the battle against inflation.* This could happen if observed reductions in the overall inflation rate, combined with growing concern over the social and economic effects of the recession, should lead to relaxation of the degree of demand restraint needed to overcome inflation in the long run. Such a policy would be very shortsighted. But there is also a risk in allowing economic activity to decline to so depressed a level—without a reasonable cushioning of the effects of the decline and the prospect of an early recovery—that productive investment will be seriously discouraged. Moreover, the economic hardships and social tensions that may result could produce powerful political pressures for excessively strong countermeasures to recession.

Although we strongly support carefully targeted measures to cushion the adverse effects of recession on those least able to bear them, we believe that sustained adherence to firm restraint in fiscal and monetary policies is essential to effectively reduce the underlying inflation rate. In particular, it is vital to avoid excessive restimulation of the economy or other kinds of antirecessionary actions that could again cause inflation to accelerate.

---

*See memorandum by ROBERT R. NATHAN, page 19.

We believe that giving first-priority attention to demand restraint need not be incompatible with other steps that contribute to the long-term attack on underlying inflation and that are vitally necessary to rebuilding a healthy economy. *Indeed, unless the current period of economic slack is used aggressively to begin a sustained attack on the longer-term forces that aggravate inflation by increasing production costs and eroding productivity, the sacrifices associated with demand restraint will turn out to have been largely wasted, and the subsequent recovery from the recession would be followed by an even worse inflation than we have recently experienced.*

We must begin *now* to correct the biases accumulated in our economy over many years that discourage productive investment and saving. **As part of a long-range strategy, basic public policies should be redirected so that a greater share of a growing real gross national product (GNP) will be devoted to saving, investment, and innovation.** We need to seize the current opportunity to modernize our existing industrial capacity, develop new high-technology industries, improve our competitive ability both here and abroad, allow market forces to restructure chronically noncompetitive firms and industries, stimulate greater price competitiveness, preserve and increase our agricultural productivity, and reverse the decline in nonagricultural productivity. These objectives should be pursued in ways that strengthen and enlarge the role of the market system. **The focus should be on achieving an economic recovery that is compatible with a sustainable long-term restoration of a growing, competitive economy.**

U.S. tax laws contain major disincentives to saving, capital investment, and innovation. Reforms to help remedy this situation, such as provisions for more rapid capital recovery allowances, should be adopted promptly and programmed over a number of years within prudent overall budgetary limits. Efforts to reduce U.S. dependence on foreign energy sources must be intensified. Faster progress needs to be made in removing regulatory and other disincentives that lead to unwarranted upward price pressures and restrict growth without commensurate social benefits. Regulatory reform has been talked about for years, but actions to date have fallen far short of what is required.

We make no claim that the proposals offered in this statement cover *all* the steps needed to end inflation and restore healthy economic growth. We believe that the steps recommended are necessary but that they may not be sufficient. For this reason, this Committee intends to continue to give priority attention to the inflation process.*

Our nation has no experience in judging how the economy will respond to policy measures at the current high underlying inflation rates. We

---

*See memorandum by JACK F. BENNETT, page 19.

do know, however, that our economy has developed a severe inflationary bias that has become deeply imbedded in a wide range of institutional arrangements and in public attitudes. In particular, structural rigidities have made our economic system much more resistant to downward than to upward pressures on wages and prices so that temporary price spurts in commodity markets or other price-raising "shocks" to the system are often transformed into more permanent wage-price increases.

Thus, much more systematic thought needs to be given to the mechanisms that either aggravate the spiraling of inflation once it has gotten under way or reduce the effectiveness of traditional demand restraint measures in unwinding wage-price spirals. **In particular, there is need for a thorough reappraisal of present practices that involve full or partial indexation of wages and other income payments to cost-of-living increases.*** Any reappraisal should, of course, be sensitive to equity considerations and make due allowance for the special needs of persons with very modest incomes and no possibilities for added earnings.

However, we remain opposed to mandatory wage and price controls during peacetime.** Aside from the monumental enforcement problems they create, such controls seriously impair incentives, distort the rational allocation of resources by the private market system, and are likely to damage rather than improve long-term prospects for price stability and economic growth.

The policies we advocate will inevitably entail temporary hardships and sacrifices for all groups and economic sectors. Although concentration of these burdens on those least able to bear them can, and should, be avoided by appropriately targeted transfer payments, the gains resulting from such temporary sacrifices will in time work to the benefit of all groups in our society.*****

A sound economy, with high levels of productivity and private employment, is fundamental to solving most of the other problems this country faces. It is central to our strength in foreign policy and international trade, to our national security, and to the achievement of our domestic social and political goals. Healthy cities, adequate job opportunities and upward mobility, security in old age, a clean environment, quality education, strong cultural institutions—all depend on a highly productive, competitive, low-inflation economy.

In the end, our political freedoms and the future of our democratic society depend on our ability to achieve sustained real economic growth without inflation and to give our citizens and other nations around the world the confidence that the United States will succeed in this endeavor.

---

*See memoranda by JACK F. BENNETT and by FRAZAR B. WILDE, page 20.

**See memorandum by JACK F. BENNETT, page 20.

***See memorandum by JOHN H. FILER, page 20.

DEVELOPING AN ECONOMIC STRATEGY

A strategy for fighting inflation and rebuilding a sound economy should give special attention to four basic points.

First, both the public at large and our political leaders must clearly grasp the long-term nature of the nation's economic problems and take prompt and determined action to deal with them. Many of today's short-term issues are, in fact, the neglected long-range issues of five, ten, or fifteen years ago.* Actions aimed at short-range problems must be placed in a long-range context. Decision makers must carefully balance short- and long-term considerations in instances where these conflict. An example is decontrol of energy prices, which contributes to short-term increases in the consumer price index but fosters long-term energy conservation and supply growth.** Moreover, government needs to convey its long-term policy intentions to the public in a clear and credible fashion. This is essential for reversing inflationary expectations. Investors, managers, consumers, and wage earners need to know what to expect from government over a sufficient number of years to permit sound decisions on long-term efforts. "Stop and go" economic policies are a prescription for economic failure.

Second, domestic economic policies must be consistent with international reality.*** There must be a recognition that the domestic economy is only one component of the larger world economy. Some domestic issues, such as energy and national defense, are driven by external forces beyond our complete control. We must also be competitive in the world marketplace; otherwise, we will achieve neither our foreign policy objectives nor our domestic economic, social, and political goals.

Third, we need to develop a broadly based political consensus to achieve a sound economy.**** A strong, competitive economy is a common denominator in meeting the needs of the many diverse constituencies in our society that are often in apparent opposition—businesses (large and small), labor, minorities, consumers, the elderly, environmentalists, the generally disadvantaged. All these groups depend on the resources that ultimately come from a productive economy. This fundamental fact needs to be understood by all sectors of American society, including the disadvantaged, and accepted as a reason for supporting public policies that will create such an economy.**** For equally compelling reasons of humanity and equity, national policy can, and should, give weight to the concerns of those disadvantaged members of our society who have the greatest need.

Fourth, the national economic strategy should include multiple interrelated measures applied over an extended time period. The nation's economic problems are interconnected and have many common roots. They

---

*See memorandum by EMILIO G. COLLADO, page 21.

**See memorandum by ROBERT R. NATHAN, page 21.

***See memorandum by WILLIAM F. MAY, page 21.

****See memoranda by E. L. MCNEELY, page 22.

result from several decades of failure to deal effectively with basic long-range economic issues. We should therefore not expect them to be resolved quickly, as separate issues, or by timid measures. Taken simultaneously, certain policy actions can serve several related purposes.

With this background, we now turn to specific elements of the needed multifaceted strategy.[2]

FIGHTING INFLATION: THE CENTRAL ROLE OF DEMAND RESTRAINT*

Firm and sustained adherence to a policy of required restraint on total demand through monetary and fiscal actions is essential to reducing inflation. Monetary and fiscal policies should be balanced and mutually supporting. In the past, anti-inflation action has often lacked balance, placing too much of the burden on monetary restraint and too little on fiscal discipline.

Over the long run, fiscal and monetary policies should foster a relatively moderate but steady advance in economic activity geared to the growth in the economy's long-term potential real output.

Unfortunately—but unavoidably—the policy of restraint is likely to be accompanied by a substantially higher degree of economic slack over the near term than is needed or tolerable over the longer run. Nevertheless, as the recession continues, policy makers must not yield to the temptation to abandon monetary restraint or government spending limits. We recognize that deficits during periods of recession and early in the recovery can be appropriate to the extent that they reflect the workings of the budget's automatic stabilizers, such as unemployment insurance payments and income tax receipts, in response to weakness in overall economic activity. However, even if some adjustments should be needed in the overall stance of monetary and fiscal policies beyond the workings of the automatic stabilizers, we should strive for a policy of firm limits on monetary growth and government expenditures.** (For further discussion, see pages 10–11.)

Under present circumstances, monetary policy should continue to be directed primarily at fostering moderate rates of monetary and credit expansion. With a more disciplined fiscal policy, this monetary posture can lead, in due course, to some additional reductions in interest rates.

---

[2]/CED's Research and Policy Committee has previously issued a succession of in-depth policy statements on inflation and healthy economic growth, most recently *The Economy in 1977–78: Strategy for an Enduring Expansion* (1976), *Fighting Inflation and Promoting Growth* (1976), and *High Employment Without Inflation: A Positive Program for Economic Stabilization* (1972). The present statement builds upon those principles in these earlier statements that have stood the test of time, with the analysis extended and modified to take more recent developments into account.

---

*See memorandum by ROBERT R. NATHAN, page 22.

**See memorandum by NORMA PACE, page 22.

On the budgetary side, it is particularly important to assure sustained commitment to greater fiscal discipline and improved control over federal expenditures. It is imperative that all categories of the budget be subject to intensive review at regular intervals.

We consider it essential, however, that efforts to achieve budgetary discipline be carried out in a way that is consistent with the long-term measures needed to strengthen productivity, reduce inflation, and expand total real output and incomes. In particular, we believe that even within the context of a tight budget, provisions need to be made for incentives for more rapid capital recovery, encouraging innovation and research and development outlays, stimulating high-risk entrepreneurial investment, and fostering improved skill training for the unemployed and underemployed.

We are aware that to accomplish this objective, other projected budgetary outlays must be trimmed, even if the recommended measures are phased in over a period of time to spread out their budgetary impact. This will be an especially hard task in view of the compelling demands of the nation's energy and defense programs. *Thus, healthy long-range real economic growth is essential.* Such growth is needed to provide the fiscal resources to cover all these partially competing requirements within a viable political framework.

Improved fiscal management requires more than concentration on the officially defined federal budget for a single year. If control over expenditures is to be effective, budgetary planning needs to be conducted on a multiyear basis. As part of this process, a determined effort must be made to move toward a phased reduction of the share of government spending in the GNP. Particular care needs to be taken that transfer payments intended to alleviate hardships are, in fact, channeled only to individuals and groups in genuine need. Off-budget items, including federal credit and loan guarantee programs, must be brought under closer control.

Tax changes, similarly, should be devised in a long-term framework. Federal tax receipts typically go through wider swings than expenditures do as inflation automatically boosts tax payments and recession curtails them. Changes beyond these automatic responses might well be needed in coming years. For example, reductions in tax rates may at some point be justified to offset inflation-induced increases in the effective tax burden, to reduce tax disincentives to saving and investment, or to counter recession (see page 10). There can also be a case for shifting the relative burdens imposed by different types of taxes to further some of these objectives. Conversely, a tax rate increase (or at least, forgone tax rate reductions) could become necessary to finance heavier defense expenditures (see page 17) or as an added brake on inflation if other policies should not suffice.

It is not the purpose of this statement to propose a specific program of tax changes for calendar year 1981 and beyond.* We urge, however, that decisions with respect to possible tax policy changes that would become effective next year be based on the following guiding principles.

If corrective fiscal measures to affect the overall course of the economy should be needed in addition to automatic stabilizers, such measures should be (and we believe can be) concentrated on tax changes that contribute directly over the longer run to the two basic goals of reducing inflation and rebuilding a sound economy.

We believe that there is an urgent need for tax reforms that will reduce disincentives to capital investment and increase long-term incentives for individual saving.** (For a further discussion, see pages 11–13.) Such reforms are needed whether or not any statutory action is taken to ease the scheduled rise in the effective overall tax burden next year. Indeed, the present period of economic slack presents a special opportunity for stimulating capital investment aimed at revitalizing the nation's stock of productive equipment, developing new products, and achieving lower costs and greater productivity. In order not to stimulate inflation, tax changes to foster such capital investment should be designed to phase in any net federal revenue losses gradually within prudent overall budget limits. If such phased reductions are legislated now and made permanent, we believe they will have an immediate effect on decisions to expand capital investment, even before such reductions become fully effective.

Since a significant increase in the effective tax burden on individuals is currently scheduled for calendar year 1981, moderate corrective tax action to achieve the purposes outlined in the foregoing paragraphs need not be in conflict with the prescription for continuing fiscal restraint. Without such tax action, there could actually be a significant shift toward increased fiscal restriction next year, mainly because of an estimated increase of $40 to $50 billion in the effective tax burden that will result from the inflation-induced "upcreep" in income tax brackets, the scheduled rise in social security taxes, and other factors.[3]

---

[3]/ This estimated increase in the effective tax burden in the next calendar year relates to changes in tax receipts from 1980 to 1981 under assumed nonrecession (high-employment) conditions in both years that can be expected to result from increases in *effective tax rates* (including those resulting from bracket upcreep and a higher base for social security tax computations) and from newly imposed taxes. This differs from the projected total increase in actual receipts in fiscal year 1981, which, according to the midyear budget review, is estimated at $86 billion. The estimate used in the text also does not take into account the facts that the real value of both personal and corporate incomes will have been further eroded by inflation and that a substantial part of the capital appreciation subject to taxation will have resulted from inflation.

---

*See memorandum by NORMA PACE, page 23.

**See memorandum by E. L. MCNEELY, page 23.

Actual decisions on possible tax actions affecting 1981 cannot, however, be based solely on the prospective rise in the overall tax burden. They must also take full account of the prospective level of economic activity and the likely future trend in government expenditures. In particular, any large and rapid increase in outlays for national defense must be offset by expenditure cuts elsewhere and by actions to assure adequate overall tax revenues.

It is essential, therefore, that any easing of the prospective overall tax burden in 1981 be contingent on determined action to assure adequate restraint on total expenditures.* Indeed, tax and expenditure programs affecting 1981 and subsequent years must be consistent with the goal of achieving a surplus in the federal budget as high employment is restored. Moreover, specific new tax actions should be designed to further the longer-run goal of gradually reducing the total share of GNP taken by taxes, in balance with a phased reduction in government spending as a share of GNP.

Although demand policies are central to reducing inflation, they will not by themselves restore the economy to a sound condition. Demand restraint must not become so severe that it blocks out necessary incentives for capital formation and productivity growth, which can also make a contribution to reducing inflation in the long run and which are vital to restoring real economic growth and increasing job formation.**

As part of a longer-range strategy, the basic fiscal-monetary mix needs to be shifted so that a greater share of a growing real GNP will be devoted to saving, investment, and innovation. Additional policies that can help achieve this goal are outlined in the next section.

RESTORING PRODUCTIVITY AND REAL ECONOMIC GROWTH

To increase productivity and restore real economic growth in this country, there is an urgent need to reduce disincentives and, where necessary, strengthen incentives for private investment and saving. As we noted earlier, vigorous real growth is essential to providing the resources needed to meet all the demands on the nation's output.

We need a *national policy for private investment* that would permit more rapid capital recovery, encourage high-risk entrepreneurial investment and innovation, and foster improved skill training. Such a policy should make effective use of constructive public-private partnerships where they are needed, but its major focus should be on investment within and by the private sector. It should draw, to the fullest extent possible, on the strength and initiative of private business and on the benefits of the competitive market system.

---

*See memorandum by JAMES Q. RIORDAN, page 23.

**See memorandum by ROBERT R. NATHAN, page 24.

A central part of a national policy for private investment should be the reduction of disincentives to investment in new plant and equipment. There is ample evidence that since 1973, a low rate of private capital formation has been a major contributor to this country's dismal productivity record. Yet, the United States is relatively more dependent on the private sector for investment in expansion and modernization of productive capacity than many of its international competitors. A significant increase in the rate of U.S. private capital formation is necessary both to support healthy rates of productivity gain and real economic growth and to meet the growing capital needs arising from such factors as increased energy costs, more stringent environmental and safety standards, and an accumulation of obsolete plant and equipment.

Not only has the lag in capital investment contributed to rising inflation and U.S. losses in international competitiveness, but high rates of inflation have, in turn, been a major force in reducing the rate of replacement of obsolete plant and equipment. This has happened because allowable depreciation of existing plant and equipment is based on historical costs, which, in a period of rapid inflation, are much lower than replacement costs.

We believe that a very important action to stimulate investment in new plant and equipment would be the prompt introduction of more rapid capital recovery allowances.* A substantial shortening of depreciation schedules would, in our view, be the most practical first step toward removing major existing disincentives to capital investment.[4] We believe this change can, and should, be achieved within a disciplined overall budget.

Stepped-up investment incentives also constitute the most important measure we can take to *foster more rapid technological progress.* In a recent policy statement,[5] we highlighted the need for added incentives to encourage a high level of private investment in high-risk ventures that lead to innovation and its diffusion throughout the economy. In addition, we recommended a shift to "flexible depreciation" of equipment and structures used for research and development, major reforms to make the patent system more efficient and effective, and increased government support for basic research.

---

[4] Permitting more rapid capital recovery allowances does not constitute an unconditional tax *reduction* for business; it is, rather, a tax *deferral* that helps to reduce the inflationary erosion of corporate funds available for replacement of plant and equipment. Such a tax deferral is, of course, valuable to the tax-paying business firm and can be extended so long as the firm achieves and maintains an accelerated rate of new capital investment that fully matches its higher level of tax-deductible annual depreciation charges.

---

[5] See *Stimulating Technological Progress* (1980).

---

*See memorandum by RODERICK M. HILLS, page 24.

The changes we have recommended to encourage investment will help to generate the added private savings that will be needed in due course to finance such investment on a noninflationary basis. We believe, however, that additional tax revisions aimed at longer-run saving and investment trends would be desirable over time for two reasons: to motivate people to raise their personal savings targets gradually as economic expansion progresses and to encourage both businesses of all sizes and individuals *to channel more of their savings into equity investment in productive enterprises.* Measures that increase the base of equity investment relative to debt financing, particularly in smaller businesses, will add to the financial stability of business firms, help them to grow more rapidly, and increase their entrepreneurial potential.

A good example of a constructive tax change for these purposes would be an additional permanent reduction in the tax rate levied on capital gains on equity investments. The revenue loss from a lower percentage tax rate should be at least partially (or perhaps even completely) offset by the greater volume of capital transactions likely to materialize as a result of a smaller tax disincentive.

However, the most constructive encouragement to saving and productive investment will come from the orderly reduction of inflation. Our stubbornly high inflation rate is the biggest single disincentive to saving.

PROVIDING VITAL JOB OPPORTUNITIES

We must also give attention to developing job opportunities in order to achieve the higher levels of productive employment that are a requirement for a healthy economy and a free society. Incentives for private saving and investment needed to support greater capital formation can themselves be important long-run contributors to job formation and higher employment levels. To begin with, workers are needed to build the new capital equipment and to put it in place. Within an appropriate monetary and fiscal environment, such new capital equipment, once installed, can enhance productivity, reduce per-unit costs, and increase sales both at home and abroad, thereby opening the door to greater expansion of output and increased employment. Further benefits can result from training and job redesign to make members of the labor force more productive, particularly when such efforts are carried out by the private sector. Appropriately tailored training and recruitment can also help prevent skill shortages and labor supply bottlenecks, both of which can aggravate inflation.

However, these and other longer-run job-creating forces will for a time be outweighed by the cyclical rise in joblessness resulting from the current recession. The resulting burden on the individuals thus unemployed is lightened in varying degrees by the array of public and private income supports already in place. It is equitable and right for society to use such measures to limit the hardship imposed upon people who lose their jobs (although benefits should not be made so large that they become a desirable alternative to work). At the same time, we believe it would be imprudent to launch major new projects for public employment as antirecession measures. All too often, such projects turn out to be too late, relatively unproductive, and so costly and difficult to terminate that they aggravate inflationary forces in the ensuing recovery, thereby weakening the permanent job-creating strength of the economy.

However, specially targeted measures are needed and should be directed to the *structurally unemployed,* who are outside the reach of normal job-formation processes.* **In particular, a major public-private partnership is called for to involve businesses (both large and small) much more actively in efforts to provide skill training and productive jobs for the structurally unemployed and underemployed and to foster a better transition from school to work.**[6] In addition, we believe there is a major need for increased private-sector concern with improved skill training and upgrading of its own regular work force.

The economy can also achieve higher productivity by drawing more effectively on the combined resources and ingenuity of the private sector. In particular, a greater effort is required to develop local labor-management committees that will work independently (or in cooperation with the public sector) to foster constructive approaches to raising productivity and improving the ability of the United States to compete in international markets.

INCREASING THE EFFECTIVENESS OF THE MARKET ECONOMY

Underlying all of the nation's economic goals is the need to restore and maintain a vigorous competitive market system.[7] *The proliferation of unnecessary or overly burdensome government regulations has interfered too*

---

[6] See CED's policy statement *Jobs for the Hard-to-Employ: New Directions for a Public-Private Partnership* (1978) for specific policy recommendations to develop such a partnership. Action along these lines has recently been launched through the Private Sector Initiative Program under Title VII of the Comprehensive Employment and Training Act (CETA) and the Targeted Jobs Tax Credit, with the National Alliance of Business taking a leadership role within the business community in implementing these efforts.

---

[7] See *Redefining Government's Role in the Market System* (1979) for our detailed analysis and recommendations.

---

*See memorandum by ROY L. ASH, page 24.

much with the natural forces of the marketplace. Excessive and ineffective government regulations—federal, state, and local—have contributed significantly to the current inflation and sometimes to production cutbacks and job losses. Such regulations not only add directly to both business and government costs but can also push up the inflation rate and depress real output by adversely affecting investment and productivity, discouraging innovation, and depriving individual firms as well as the economy of needed flexibility to respond effectively to changing conditions.

It is urgent that comprehensive measures be adopted to bring regulatory decisions and practices under closer scrutiny and stricter discipline with a view to assuring greater scope for competitive market processes. Regulatory management and coordination need to be improved, with particular attention given to fostering a more predictable and stable long-term investment climate, defining regulatory objectives and specifications more clearly, evaluating both the benefits and the costs of regulation, eliminating or reducing unnecessary regulation, substituting performance standards for detailed design specifications in regulations, utilizing economic incentives and disincentives in preference to mandatory directives, and providing for periodic reviews of existing regulations.

We also believe that a continued basic U.S. commitment to liberal trade and investment policies consistent with national security requirements is vitally important for the success of the anti-inflation effort and for enhancing U.S. productivity and competitiveness over the long run. Although there are instances in which discriminatory foreign trade practices threaten serious disruptions in particular U.S. markets and may justify countervailing actions, the principal response to foreign competition should be to make U.S. industries more modern and productive and to allow for flexibility in shifting resources to their most efficient uses. At the same time, the government should insist that existing obligations under international trade and related agreements be scrupulously observed by all signatories and that domestic rules in such fields as antitrust policy take full account of the fact that U.S. firms frequently operate in intensely competitive worldwide markets.

In other ways, too, there is need to reduce rigidities, especially those related to wages and prices, and to eliminate restrictive practices that interfere with sound competition and economic efficiency.* Particularly important are steps to reduce impediments to technological progress created by unreasonable government requirements, business practices, and union rules; curtailment of uneconomic price subsidies and output restrictions; actions to overcome racial and other forms of discrimination and to allow

---

*See memorandum by FRAZAR B. WILDE, page 25.

free entry and exit of firms and workers into and from particular industries and occupations; improved formulation and enforcement of the antitrust laws to focus sharply on competitive economic efficiency and on U.S. ability to compete effectively overseas; and efforts to make price- and wage-setting processes more responsive to changes in demand. Finally, we must avoid subsidies to companies or industries that have become chronically noncompetitive.

We recognize that energetic steps to strengthen competition and increase the effectiveness of the market system may in some instances impose special burdens on particular groups least able to bear them, such as poor and elderly persons. These instances can call for special ameliorative actions, but such actions should normally take the form of direct transfer payments to those in need, rather than government interference with the workings of the price system in particular markets.

TWO ISSUES OF SPECIAL CONCERN: ENERGY AND DEFENSE

Two special issues of vital strategic and national security concern are also highly important from the viewpoint of inflation and long-term growth.

One of these issues is *energy*. Ensuring uninterrupted energy supplies during the balance of this century and beyond is a problem of massive proportions for the United States and its major allies. In addition, the plain facts are that energy is going to cost much more than it does now and that there will be significant changes in the mix of energy sources used in this country. These developments will cause some disruptions. If the nation is to adjust to these changing circumstances with a minimum of risk to the economic and social order, we must be clear about the key components of a national energy program.[8]

The United States must intensify its efforts to reduce its dependence on foreign energy sources. At the same time, it must preserve and protect access—both for this country and for nations friendly to it—to the substantial level of energy imports that will still be vital for many years to come. Such actions are crucial not only for strategic national security rea-

---

[8]/For detailed accounts of CED's policy recommendations, see *Key Elements of a National Energy Strategy* (1977) and *Helping Insure Our Energy Future: A Program for Developing Synthetic Fuel Plants Now* (1979).

sons but also for the efficient long-term performance of the economy and for the containment of inflationary pressures.

Equally strong emphasis must be placed on conserving energy and on expanding the usable supplies of domestic energy resources, including not only oil and gas but also coal and nuclear power. The private investment needed to accomplish this, starting immediately and extending over a period of decades, is enormous.

In our view, the most important means for achieving these objectives is *action to encourage maximum feasible reliance on free market forces* in production, distribution, and consumption. The price system must be allowed to work effectively, both to achieve conservation and to increase supply. That means, among other measures, removing unworkable and inappropriate allocation and regulatory requirements and expediting environmental and other regulatory decisions. There must be an energy investment climate that is reasonably stable over the expected life of necessary major long-term investments.

Moreover, there can be no solution of the longer-term (beyond twenty years) energy problem unless we *begin now with the early steps of the massive task of developing new sources of energy.* We need to remove disincentives and strengthen incentives for the very large private-sector investment necessary to finance research and commercial-scale development of synthetic fuels and solar power as well as other renewable energy sources.*

The second issue of special concern is *national defense.* Consideration of what constitutes an adequate level of defense expenditures is beyond the scope of this policy statement. **However, it is vital to assure adequate, non-inflationary financing of whatever increases in defense outlays may be deemed essential to national security in the years immediately ahead.** Aggressive steps need to be taken to manage current programs more effectively and to eliminate marginal programs and unnecessary expenditures. Even after such steps are taken, however, the need for increased outlays may be substantial. The resources required for national defense must be carefully projected over a period of years and clearly fitted into a budget framework that maintains the steady fiscal discipline needed to control inflation and restore real economic growth. Of course, some military needs cannot be foreseen, but that should be no excuse for failure to plan and pay for regular and foreseeable military requirements in a fiscally responsible manner. In terms of added inflation, the price of failing to do so can be high indeed.

---

*See memorandum by EMILIO G. COLLADO, page 25.

CONCLUDING COMMENTS

The proposals offered in this statement are not intended to cover *all* the measures needed to end inflation and restore healthy economic growth. We believe them to be necessary, but they may not be sufficient. Productivity gains, for example, will not result in reduced inflation if excessive wage increases or other excessive income claims prevent a significant part of the productivity gains from being translated into lower prices. Considerably more thought needs to be devoted to possible ways of preventing such excessive claims and, more generally, of modifying the processes that lead to a spiraling of inflation. This Committee intends to continue to give priority attention to the inflation process, including ways of developing an improved consensus among the various groups in American society regarding the policies most conducive to noninflationary economic growth.*

We do not believe, however, that the country can afford to relax the attack on inflation or to postpone forceful action to restore a strong, competitive economy until a full consensus on solutions for all aspects of the problem has been developed. A realistic opportunity now exists to secure agreement on those key steps toward a solution of the problems that we have outlined in this statement. We are convinced that adoption of these steps, if carried out in the framework of a cohesive long-term strategy, would constitute a major contribution to restoring a growing, noninflationary economy.

---

*See memorandum by ROBERT B. SEMPLE, page 25.

Memoranda of Comment, Reservation, or Dissent

Page 4, by ROBERT R. NATHAN, with which ROBERT B. SEMPLE has asked to be associated

There is perhaps a greater risk of ignoring the underlying causes of inflation and relying overwhelmingly on the recession to bring about a marked and sustained decline in the rate of inflation. Of course, a massive recovery program could terminate even a temporary abatement of inflation, but stonewalling recovery measures and urging that a long and costly recession is the only answer to inflation will in time lead to just such massive recovery programs. Excess demand should be avoided during the recovery, but fruitless unemployment and recession should be abhorred because they will not bring a trade-off in much lower inflation. A suitable recovery program can be designed so that it meets anti-inflationary objectives as well as recovery.

Page 5, by JACK F. BENNETT, with which EMILIO G. COLLADO has asked to be associated

While I have not voted against this statement in its present form, I feel that it puts CED under a serious obligation to pursue the subject of inflation until the Committee reaches specific conclusions of more practical benefit than the generalities in this paper. For example, the statement advocates a tax cut next year to streamline investment through provisions for more rapid capital recovery even though "other projected budgetary outlays must be trimmed. . . ." I agree with this recommendation as far as it goes, but it does not seem to me that the recommendation is meaningful or that CED has done its job until the Committee indicates the areas in which it believes those cuts should be made. I am also concerned that some of the statement's generalities, particularly those on page 10, could be read as recommending additional tax cuts in 1981, beyond those made possible by expenditure cuts, because of scheduled increases in effective tax rates next year. Given the large size of the forecast deficit for next year, a year of forecast recovery, I believe such a recommendation would be in serious conflict with the report's basic prescription of sufficient fiscal restraint to ensure continuous gradual reduction in inflation.

Page 6, by JACK F. BENNETT, with which EMILIO G. COLLADO has asked to be associated

By its expression of apparent opposition to indexation, the Committee seems to me to be, unwisely, advocating that a reduction in some economic groups' shares in the national income be sought through the arbitrary effects of inflation rather than through the conscious adoption of appropriate policies.

Page 6, by FRAZAR B. WILDE, with which C. WREDE PETERSMEYER and ROBERT B. SEMPLE have asked to be associated

The attack on inflation needs to observe the continuous increase in costs for those labor settlements which involve indexing. We need either by renegotiation or by federal action to control this serious increase in cost of production.

Page 6, by JACK F. BENNETT, with which ROY L. ASH, FLETCHER L. BYROM, and EMILIO G. COLLADO have asked to be associated

It seems to me that the Committee should also recognize that "voluntary" wage and price guidelines have the same types of deleterious effects as mandatory controls.

Page 6, by JOHN H. FILER, with which FLETCHER L. BYROM has asked to be associated

This excellent policy statement would be more effective and complete if it did not fail to acknowledge the existing and potential role of the non-profit "third sector" in this country. This omission is particularly noticeable in the material on this page and on pages 7 and 16.

A myriad of voluntary organizations exist to help ameliorate the burdens on people such as the poor and the elderly. These organizations cannot eliminate the burdens entirely but should be encouraged, by government policy and private initiative, in an attempt to do so. To imply that the only available resource is "direct transfer payments" is a mistake. Individual, corporate, and institutional philanthropy is an essential part of the long-term process to produce and maintain a healthy, non-inflationary, equitable economy and society.

As a matter of fact, I believe that a substantially increased corporate effort to prevent the temporary hardships, acknowledged in this paper, from falling on those least able to bear them would help over time to create a climate in which the recommendations of the paper would be more likely to be adopted.

Page 7, by EMILIO G. COLLADO, with which ROY L. ASH has asked to be associated

The issues were not "neglected" issues of the earlier years but the results of positive actions, mostly of government, which have gone a long way toward ruining a rather well-functioning economy.

Page 7, by ROBERT R. NATHAN, with which ROBERT B. SEMPLE has asked to be associated

Significant growth in the supply of oil in response to higher oil prices is highly doubtful. Much more conservation in the use of oil is essential, but this can best be achieved by high excise taxes on gasoline and perhaps other petroleum products. If the country waits for substantially higher gasoline prices to result in the marketplace, we are likely to have much less conservation than if a substantial tax is promptly imposed on gasoline. Equally or perhaps more important is the fact that large revenues from sizable taxes on gasoline could be used to lower the rates of inflation by reducing state and local excise and sales taxes and perhaps payroll taxes as well. If gasoline prices rise only through the marketplace, there will be no such revenues which the government can use to offset the impact of higher gasoline prices on total inflation. Finally, higher gasoline and other petroleum product prices that reflect the increased taxes will encourage alternative sources of energy just as effectively as higher oil prices determined by the oil companies.

Page 7, by WILLIAM F. MAY

I want to elaborate on the recommendation that "domestic economic policies must be consistent with international reality." Part of that reality is the development of free trade, which is consistent with CED's past and present policy. Fair trade and the Tokyo Round were small steps in this direction. Much has yet to be done to ensure free trade among the several markets of our trading partners. This will necessitate the further elimination of nontariff barriers such as inspection procedures, specifications, etc., as well as nonmarket financial support of foreign industries by the governments of those countries.

I believe that this is an important aspect of a realistic appraisal of international trade and relates directly to the control of inflation by most efficient and economic manufacture from whatever international source, as well as the fair preservation of our markets for our work force.

Page 7, by E.L. MCNEELY

It is difficult to define what a political consensus is and to identify it even if we were to achieve it, unless the congressional voting record is to be the criterion. Public consensus is another matter.

Page 7, by E.L. MCNEELY

The "disadvantaged" will not accept public policies that will not clearly improve their lot short term.

Page 8, by ROBERT R. NATHAN, with which ROBERT B. SEMPLE has asked to be associated

The degree of emphasis placed on demand restraint is excessive. Demand restraint, as in the last two recessions, will likely bring a temporary drop in the rate of inflation, but sooner or later recovery may bring even worse rates of inflation. The other roles indicated in this report, dealing with productivity, investment, trade policies, competition, tax changes, and the like, are very important factors that should be aggressively pursued in the war on inflation. They are not just "goodies;" they are basic issues which must be given high priority if we are to achieve a significant and continuing reduction of inflation.

Page 8, by NORMA PACE, with which FLETCHER L. BYROM has asked to be associated

Ignored in the discussion of monetary policy and the setting of appropriate targets for either money supply or interest rates is the impact of velocity, that is, the rate of use of money, on economic activity. If political and economic events were to dim business and consumer confidence further, the restraining effect of modest increases in money supply will be exacerbated by a decline in the rate of use of the smaller amount of available money. Conversely, even with a small increase in money supply, greater velocity can carry activity to even higher levels. Monetarists admit that velocity cannot be controlled, but money supply can. However, that should not lead to the neglect of its impact; the management of money cannot be confined so exclusively to the supply (or its companion, interest rates) in the light of this deficiency. Federal Reserve authorities should recognize this weakness in their approach and maintain a more flexible attitude toward monetary policies than is indicated by insistence on adherence to specific numerical targets.

Page 10, by NORMA PACE, with which FLETCHER L. BYROM has asked to be associated

An estimated deficit of $30 to $40 billion in fiscal 1981 will be caused primarily by recession. It will occur despite a $40-billion increase in revenues resulting from new taxes. Tax liabilities will also rise rapidly because of "bracket creep," namely, the movement of people into higher income brackets where tax rates rise. This is an unusual situation requiring special analysis and careful evaluation of timing. Programs have been proposed for broad-based, phased-in tax cuts that border on tax reform which could be initiated on a small scale as early as 1981 and would escalate with time. They would be funded by growth as these tax programs and the expectation of tax changes take hold and encourage balanced growth in both demand and supply.

Page 10, by E.L. MCNEELY

To some extent I question the emphasis throughout the paper on taxes. Perhaps more emphasis should have been given to productivity and labor-management relations than the one paragraph on page 14.

Page 11, by JAMES Q. RIORDAN

I agree with the statement but believe that the recommendation for early enactment of tax cuts to stimulate investment should be unconditional. Tax cuts designed to increase investment need to be made immediately and should not be contingent upon spending cuts. Spending cuts are needed, but improving the investment climate should not be contingent upon the timing of our success in controlling expenditures. A competitive, productive private economy is essential if we are to reduce deficits and control inflation over the long term.

Page 11, by ROBERT R. NATHAN, with which FLETCHER L. BYROM and ROBERT B. SEMPLE have asked to be associated

Recessions are often counterproductive in the war on inflation. Higher interest rates early in a recession tend to be inflationary. More serious is the decline in capacity utilization which depresses productivity and pushes up unit costs. Over the longer run the most serious consequence of a recession is the decline it brings about in the levels of private investment. What this country desperately needs is more, not less, investment in order to modernize and expand our productive capacity. As indicated in this report, incentives for investment are desirable, but the forces of recession can offset or totally negate the benefits of tax incentives in terms of encouraging private investment.

Page 12, by RODERICK M. HILLS, with which ROY L. ASH and C. WREDE PETERSMEYER have asked to be associated

On matters of tax policy, this piece, in my opinion, places undue emphasis on accelerated depreciation. It may well be that from a political standpoint, accelerated depreciation is the only relief that the business community can expect in the short run from Congress, but economic sense should not be ignored for political expediency. Tax policy deserves far more consideration than a simple new acceleration of depreciation which, at best, provides a means of indexing inflation.

To discuss depreciation without taking adequate account of the enormous economic crime created by taking capital gains in periods of rising replacement costs is to misjudge the current economic situation. We have, in effect, for several years been taxing negative income wherever the capital gains tax is on paper profits which in fact are less than inflated profits.

Page 14, by ROY L. ASH, with which C. WREDE PETERSMEYER and SIDNEY J. WEINBERG, JR., have asked to be associated

Among the most important "structural" causes of unemployment, particularly among youth, is minimum wage legislation. Such laws serve a useful social purpose, but the specific minimum pay levels established, the definitions of the included groups, and especially the lack of a "youth differential" all act to disemploy millions of people, reduce the nation's output of goods and services, add to producers' and taxpayers' costs, contribute to inflation, and create unhealthy societal tensions.

In achieving social benefits from minimum wage legislation, we've incurred major social and economic costs. Any policy considerations of structural unemployment must contend with this fact.

Page 15, by FRAZAR B. WILDE, with which C. WREDE PETERSMEYER and ROBERT B. SEMPLE have asked to be associated

I would like to make a reservation about the inflationary impact of the Davis-Bacon Act. When federal government assistance is involved, contractors are compelled to pay wage rates established by the U.S. Department of Labor which may have no relevance to the actual construction wage patterns for the locality in which the construction is taking place. We are in great need of building housing and other structures, but this law increases the costs of construction to a major extent. In addition, trades have other restrictive practices which handicap improvements and create unemployment.

Page 17, by EMILIO G. COLLADO, with which ROY L. ASH and C. WREDE PETERSMEYER have asked to be associated

I regret that the statement does not indicate that a great disincentive to energy investment is the so-called windfall profits tax.

Page 18, by ROBERT B. SEMPLE

While this is a fine statement recasting some of CED's basic suggestions for improving the economy and presenting new ones which will hopefully result in some forward steps, it is becoming distressingly more evident that to implement effectively these or any other useful programs has become next to impossible in the framework in which our government and political parties have perhaps unwittingly cast themselves. As Professor Lester C. Thurow of MIT recently wrote:

> The growth in the numbers and sophistication of interest groups has contributed to the emasculation of our political system. And we now lack the party responsibility we must have if the President and Congress are to make the tough decisions our economic situation in the world demands.

Suggestions for solving this problem do not come readily to mind, but perhaps an organization of CED's intellect and respect could perform a real service by exploring the alternatives and methods for ameliorating this fundamental deficiency without which we may never get our economic problems under control regardless of all the cures that are offered.

OBJECTIVES OF THE COMMITTEE FOR ECONOMIC DEVELOPMENT

For thirty-five years, the Committee for Economic Development has been a respected influence on the formation of business and public policy. CED is devoted to these two objectives:

To develop, through objective research and informed discussion, findings and recommendations for private and public policy which will contribute to preserving and strengthening our free society, achieving steady economic growth at high employment and reasonably stable prices, increasing productivity and living standards, providing greater and more equal opportunity for every citizen, and improving the quality of life for all.

To bring about increasing understanding by present and future leaders in business, government, and education and among concerned citizens of the importance of these objectives and the ways in which they can be achieved.

CED's work is supported strictly by private voluntary contributions from business and industry, foundations, and individuals. It is independent, nonprofit, nonpartisan, and nonpolitical.

The two hundred trustees, who generally are presidents or board chairmen of corporations and presidents of universities, are chosen for their individual capacities rather than as representatives of any particular interests. By working with scholars, they unite business judgment and experience with scholarship in analyzing the issues and developing recommendations to resolve the economic problems that constantly arise in a dynamic and democratic society.

Through this business-academic partnership, CED endeavors to develop policy statements and other research materials that commend themselves as guides to public and business policy; for use as texts in college economics and political science courses and in management training courses; for consideration and discussion by newspaper and magazine editors, columnists, and commentators; and for distribution abroad to promote better understanding of the American economic system.

CED believes that by enabling businessmen to demonstrate constructively their concern for the general welfare, it is helping business to earn and maintain the national and community respect essential to the successful functioning of the free enterprise capitalist system.

CED BOARD OF TRUSTEES

HONORARY TRUSTEES

Trustees on Leave for Government Service

STATEMENTS ON NATIONAL POLICY
ISSUED BY THE RESEARCH AND POLICY COMMITTEE

PUBLICATIONS IN PRINT

Fighting Inflation and Rebuilding a Sound Economy *(September 1980)*

Stimulating Technological Progress *(January 1980)*

Helping Insure Our Energy Future:
A Program for Developing Synthetic Fuel Plants Now *(July 1979)*

Redefining Government's Role in the Market System *(July 1979)*

Improving Management of the Public Work Force:
The Challenge to State and Local Government *(November 1978)*

Jobs for the Hard-to-Employ:
New Directions for a Public-Private Partnership *(January 1978)*

An Approach to Federal Urban Policy *(December 1977)*

Key Elements of a National Energy Strategy *(June 1977)*

The Economy in 1977-78: Strategy for an Enduring Expansion *(December 1976)*

Nuclear Energy and National Security *(September 1976)*

Fighting Inflation and Promoting Growth *(August 1976)*

Improving Productivity in State and Local Government *(March 1976)*

*International Economic Consequences of High-Priced Energy *(September 1975)*

Broadcasting and Cable Television:
Policies for Diversity and Change *(April 1975)*

Achieving Energy Independence *(December 1974)*

A New U.S. Farm Policy for Changing World Food Needs *(October 1974)*

Congressional Decision Making for National Security *(September 1974)*

*Toward a New International Economic System:
A Joint Japanese-American View *(June 1974)*

More Effective Programs for a Cleaner Environment *(April 1974)*

The Management and Financing of Colleges *(October 1973)*

Strengthening the World Monetary System *(July 1973)*

Financing the Nation's Housing Needs *(April 1973)*

Building a National Health-Care System *(April 1973)*

*A New Trade Policy Toward Communist Countries *(September 1972)*

*Statements issued in association with CED counterpart organizations in foreign countries.

CED COUNTERPART ORGANIZATIONS IN FOREIGN COUNTRIES

Close relations exist between the Committee for Economic Development and independent, nonpolitical research organizations in other countries. Such counterpart groups are composed of business executives and scholars and have objectives similar to those of CED, which they pursue by similarly objective methods. CED cooperates with these organizations on research and study projects of common interest to the various countries concerned. This program has resulted in a number of joint policy statements involving such international matters as energy, East-West trade, assistance to the developing countries, and the reduction of nontariff barriers to trade.

CE	Círculo de Empresarios *Serrano Jover 5-2°, Madrid 8, Spain*
CEDA	Committee for Economic Development of Australia *139 Macquarie Street, Sydney 2001,* *New South Wales, Australia*
CEPES	Europäische Vereinigung für Wirtschaftliche und Soziale Entwicklung *Reuterweg 14,6000 Frankfurt/Main, West Germany*
IDEP	Institut de l'Entreprise *6, rue Clément-Marot, 75008 Paris, France*
経済同友会	Keizai Doyukai (Japan Committee for Economic Development) *Japan Industrial Club Bldg.* *1 Marunouchi, Chiyoda-ku, Tokyo, Japan*
PSI	Policy Studies Institute *1-2 Castle Lane, London SW1E 6DR, England*
SNS	Studieförbundet Näringsliv och Samhälle *Sköldungagatan 2, 11427 Stockholm, Sweden*